DO NOT REMOVE
CARDS FROM POCKET

LES
CULTIVATEURS
DE
CHAMPIGNONS
DE PARIS
128, BOUL⁰ DE CHARONNE

FRANCE

The Goodness of
GARLIC

· · · · · · · · · · ·

John Midgley

Illustrated by

Ian Sidaway

RANDOM HOUSE
NEW YORK

ACKNOWLEDGEMENTS

The author thanks Vatcharin Bhumichitr for his permission to reproduce
a recipe, and Sue Midgley and Jo Swinnerton for their advice and for
checking the text.

FURTHER READING

The Food Pharmacy, by Jean Carper (Simon and Schuster); *Garlic*, by
Stephen Fulder (Thomsons); and *Superfoods*, by Michael Van Straten and
Barbara Griggs (Dorling Kindersley) are useful on the subject of garlic
and health. Reay Tannahill's *Food in History*, (Penguin) is unique and
fascinating.

Published in the United States by Random House, Inc., New York.

This work was originally published in Great Britain by
Pavilion Books Limited, London.

Library of Congress Cataloging-in-Publication Data

Midgley, John.
The goodness of garlic/John Midgley; illustrated by Ian Sidaway.
p. cm. – (The Goodness of)
ISBN 0-679-41626-9
1. Cookery (Garlic) 2. Garlic. 3. Garlic – Therapeutic use. I. Title.
TX819.G3M53 1992
641.6'526 – dc20 92-14507

Manufactured in Belgium

2 4 6 8 9 7 5 3

First U.S. edition

Contents

PART ONE
· · · · · · · · · ·

Garlic, wild garlic, giant garlic (or rocambole), elephant garlic, leeks, onions, chives, spring onions (scallions), shallots and Chinese chives all belong to the allium genus of the liliaceae (lily) group of plants, of which there are some 600 species. Most are perennial, hardy or semi-hardy, and thrive in a sunny position in well-drained soil. Alliums all share certain characteristics: bulbous, rhizomatous or fibrous rootstocks, tapering leaves growing from a bulbous base which often smell of onions when crushed, a flower-bearing stalk, and a tendency to form clumps if left undisturbed. Wild species include *allium ursinum* (ramson, or wild garlic), *allium triquetrum* (snow bell, or three-cornered garlic), *allium vineale* (crow garlic), *allium ampeloprasum* (wild leek), and *allium scorodoprasum* (giant garlic).

Garlic (*allium sativum*) and the larger but less potent elephant garlic grow easily from cloves planted at intervals of 15cm/6 inches in well-raked soil, the pointed ends facing up and only barely covered. In

northern European countries they are planted in autumn and winter and harvested in summer, although in the Mediterranean, the large, very juicy heads of new season's garlic are one of the many gustatory delights of spring. Garlic heads, whether white, red, or violet skinned, are dried and stored before consumption, but should always be eaten while the cloves still feel hard, and before they start to sprout.

Onions (*allium caepa*) come in many different shapes and sizes, from baby pickling onions to the very large yellow (or 'Spanish') onions, and the mild white and red varieties, which are particularly good as salad ingredients. Gardeners can choose one of two growing methods: either sowing seeds, which offer the widest choice of varieties, or planting sets (dormant baby bulbs). Both methods require planting in lines, in full sun. Planting times vary according to variety. Onions are ready for harvesting when the leaves yellow and begin to shrivel. Once pulled, they should be allowed to dry on the surface of the soil before being stored in a

dry, cool place. Spring onions (scallions) are the immature bulbs of yellow onions, pulled before they develop papery skins. The most popular British variety is the mildly flavoured White Lisbon. 'Welsh' or green onions are non-bulbous and grow in bunches. Like spring onions, both the shoots and the leaves of green onions are used.

Although shallots (*allium ascalonicum*) look like small onions, in reality they are closer to garlic, in that they develop not as single bulbs but as clusters of bulbs. They are easily cultivated by planting sets up to their necks in well-drained soil, in full sun. Varieties include yellow-, red- and brown-skinned shallots.

The hardy leek (*allium porrum*) is much favoured for its tolerance of cold. Like some onions, leeks are capable of attaining gigantic sizes, a quality that has long endeared them to exhibition gardeners. Usually sown from seed in spring, they can be pulled while still small and delicate, or left to mature fully and harvested in late autumn or winter. If sown late, cropping can be maintained right through the winter until early spring; traditionally leeks were a Lenten speciality in a season when few other vegetables were available. The white part of the stem is lengthened by drawing up soil around the base (blanching).

Chives (*allium schoenoprasum*) are the only pure herb of the group. They are best cultivated by planting out young plants bought in pots, or they can be sown from seed. They grow in clumps which can be divided and re-planted elsewhere. Needing virtually no further care once planted, they are an ideal garden or pot herb. Their thin, tubular leaves should be snipped with scissors or sliced with a very sharp knife, to avoid bruising. The beautiful purple flowers are also edible and make an attractive garnish in salads. Chinese chives are larger with flat leaves and are especially prized for their flower buds, which are often stir-fried.

For thousands of years, garlic has been one of the most important and widely used medicinal and folk remedies. Egyptian, Greek, Roman, Indian and Chinese physicians and herbalists recognized the many applications of garlic in treating a wide variety of conditions, even if the theoretical basis of their understanding, the presumed existence of the four natural elements of earth, air, fire and water in the body, as humours, seems bizarre today.

In the nineteenth and early part of the twentieth century, garlic became a medically prescribed drug and antiseptic. Today its remarkable therapeutic properties at last have begun to be accepted and more satisfactorily understood.

Cardiovascular disease

It is mainly in the prevention and treatment of cardiovascular disease and strokes that this recognition is taking place. In this field of medicine the powerful compounds in garlic (a pungent-smelling compound called allicin and various sulphides that it unleashes when the bulbs are crushed or cut) are understood to be effective in three ways: first, they thin the blood and help to prevent and dissolve clots and blockages in the blood vessels; secondly, they lower the level of cholesterol in the blood; and thirdly, they help to reduce blood pressure.

The old herbalists understood that garlic 'maketh subtill the blood'. The Roman physician Dioscorides observed that garlic cleared the arteries and strengthened the heart. We now understand a little of how garlic acts to slow down blood clotting and even to dissolve clots and deposits of cholesterol and fat in the blood vessels.

In the West, our diet is rich in saturated animal fats and cholesterol. These can lead to high levels of cholesterol in the blood, which is a known cause of heart disease. The condition known as *atherosclerosis* occurs when the smooth inner linings of the arteries and blood vessels become furred with fatty deposits called *plaque*. When these build up, the vessels harden, the damaged areas of the lining of the vessels (*atheromas*) attract blood clots, and the bore of the vessels narrows, leading to a potentially fatal blockage or obstruction in the circulation (*thrombosis*), and starving the surrounding tissue of oxygenated blood. If this happens in a vital artery supplying blood to the heart, the dramatic result will be a *coronary infarction*, or heart attack. Strokes may be caused by similar blockages in vessels feeding the brain.

Blockages and obstructions are also caused when fatty deposits and blood clots break loose and travel in the bloodstream to lodge in new sites. Like olive oil and aspirin, garlic and onions have anti-coagulant properties that help to prevent the formation of blood clots around fatty deposits on the vessel walls. By thinning the blood, garlic can also dissolve thromboses once they have formed and inhibit further clotting for as long as garlic is consumed.

Prolonged raised blood cholesterol increases the risk of heart disease. Blood cholesterol can be reduced by altering the diet and reducing saturated fats and cholesterol-rich foods in favour of healthy fats such as those present in oily fish and olive oil, as well as by eating garlic and onions.

A daily dose of about two cloves of garlic a day has been shown to reduce blood cholesterol by about 15 per cent. Furthermore, it would appear that garlic does not cause further reductions in people who have low levels of blood cholesterol, and that the harmful LDL (low density lipoprotein) kind of cholesterol is reduced while HDL (high density lipoprotein) cholesterol, which helps to inhibit or clear away plaques, is unaffected by garlic in the diet. Human and animal tests show that the best results are achieved when garlic is consumed regularly, and that its action in reducing cholesterol and thinning the blood ceases when the food is removed from the diet.

Finally, garlic has a mild effect in lowering blood pressure. High blood pressure is both a cause and a symptom of cardiovascular disease. The heart is put under additional strain by having to pump dense, stickier blood around the body; or, if it is forced to work harder because the blood vessels have been narrowed by atherosclerosis, the blood will flow at much higher pressure. Unlike the drugs that are prescribed to reduce blood pressure, garlic has no significant side effects. So by reducing harmful LDL cholesterol, working as an anti-coagulant, and by reducing high blood pressure, garlic is trebly effective in the prevention of heart disease.

Other benefits to health

Garlic has other remarkable properties affecting health. It is a natural antiseptic when applied externally and at one time was widely used to dress wounds. Raw garlic would be crushed and the paste spread on the lesion, then covered with bandages. It is also effective against mild bacterial infections when taken internally and was used in many countries of eastern Europe to treat conditions that synthesized medicines now deal with much more quickly and effectively, such as catarrh, asthma, bronchitis and gastroenteritis. Although antibiotics have largely replaced garlic in the treatment of infections, its potency is still widely recognized in the treatment of conditions caused by fungus and yeast, such as ringworm, candida and athlete's foot. Traditionally, raw garlic pulp is smeared on the affected areas, but eating several cloves may also be effective over a period of time.

These properties can be proven in the laboratory: Pasteur himself discovered that garlic juice killed those immediate areas of bacterial culture with which it came into contact. Fungal growths respond similarly when treated in this way. Finally, there is some evidence from disease-incidence studies in garlic-eating and garlic-abstemious populations, and from tests on laboratory animals, that its sulphur components may protect subjects against chemically induced tumours and cancers by detoxifying and dissolving these poisons, and may be effective in lowering the incidence of gastric and bowel cancers.

Onions, leeks, and chives are a little less potent but have similar therapeutic and protective properties. Although preparations such as garlic capsules, oil and powder are widely available, it would be a pity to miss the enormous gastronomic enjoyment afforded by edible alliums when they have been properly prepared and cooked. Generally, their benefits to health are not diminished by cooking. The problem of garlic on the breath can be alleviated by chewing fresh parsley, or by enjoying the company of fellow garlic-eaters!

Allium is the Latin word for garlic, transformed thus in the Romance languages: *ail* (French), *ajo* (Castilian), *al* (Catalan), and *alio* (Italian). However, the English word garlic derives from Old English gar-leac ('spear-leak', an accurate description of the plant). The words onion and *oignon* have a separate root from the Romanic names (Castilian: *cebolla*, Italian: *cipolla*): the former derive from Latin *unio*, a rustic alternative to the Latin word for onion, *caepa*, from which the latter stem. The English word leek (botanically *allium porrum*) has an Old Norse derivation in *laukr* (Dutch: *look*), whereas the Romanic names stem from the Latin *porrum* (French: *poireau*; Italian: *porro*; Castilian: *puerro*).

EDIBLE ALLIUMS IN HISTORY

The wild ancestors of garlic and onions are native to the eastern Mediterranean and Central Asia. Edible alliums are an ancient food, and their wild bulbs and shoots were collected by our earliest ancestors. When the ice sheet spread southwards, their protected, subterranean bulbs and the rhizomes of certain lilies would have afforded much-needed nourishment to beleaguered hunter-gatherers forever moving along its fringes, filling in the long gaps between the occasional bonanza of a killed woolly mammoth or a sabre-toothed tiger.

Gradually the practice of cultivating plants and cereals for food replaced nomadic foraging in certain favoured sites in the Near East, and as a consequence of that the earliest human settlements started to appear. In southern Mesopotamia, c.3000 BC, the Sumerians perfected techniques of irrigation, permitting the large-scale cultivation of garlic, onions and leeks, which with cereals, meat, and leafy vegetables formed their diet. These well-organized, agriculturally rooted settlements were the first cities.

The Old Testament (Book of Numbers) records how Moses' people pined for:

'. . . the fish, which we did eat in Egypt freely, the cucumbers, and the melons, and the leeks, and the onions, and the garlick.'

Centuries later the Greek historian Herodotus observed an inscription on The Great Pyramid recording the sums of money paid for the provisions of onions, garlic and radishes, which sustained the gangs of labourers erecting the pyramids. Garlic is depicted on the walls of ancient Egyptian tombs, and beer, bread, onions and garlic were staples for the ordinary Egyptian peasant.

The ancient Athenians are credited with the invention of *meze*, little dishes resembling hors d'oeuvres, which usually included dishes of garlic. Onions and leeks were as popular with Roman citizens as with the barbarians and peasant farmers living outside the Empire. Even the non-pastoralist nomads who roamed the great steppes behind the north shores of the Black and Caspian Seas, and lived primarily on their livestock, supplemented their carnivorous diet with plenty of onions and garlic.

After the Fall of Rome, onions continued to be grown all over Europe. In the depths of winter, when very few other crops, fish, game or livestock were available to boost and enliven the drear peasant staples of ale, cabbage, bread or gruel, onions, rich in nutrients and vitamins, were a life-saving vegetable that did much to alleviate the malnutrition from which peasants would routinely suffer at that time of year.

In the centuries after the collapse of the Roman Empire, a medical school grew up in Salerno, south of Naples, where old medical texts were translated back into Latin. Among these learned works figured commentaries on the treatises of the second-century Greek physician, Galen, themselves a rich amalgam of ideas acquired from distant lands as far afield as Persia,

India and China. The notion that diet affected health was endorsed at the Salerno medical school, and although many bizarre and now patently absurd or dangerous theories were propounded, the school correctly identified garlic's antiseptic properties and recommended it for its 'powers to save from death' while acknowledging its odour.

Meanwhile with their apothecaries, physic gardens and vegetable plots, the monastic communities continued to cultivate all manner of alliums, as medicinal and culinary herbs, and as vegetables, especially for the 200 or more meatless religious fast days in the calendar. Together with cabbage, beans and root vegetables, garlic, onions and leeks were the most commonly grown vegetables in medieval Europe.

Whereas even today the highest Hindu Brahmin caste are forbidden garlic, which they believe inflames the passions, in China, spring onions and garlic had long been appreciated by the world's most gastronomi-

cally sophisticated civilization. Passing through Yunnan in the thirteenth century, Marco Polo noted that the poor would buy animal livers at the slaughterhouse, chop them up finely and eat them raw in a garlic sauce.

The Arabs' love of food is evident from the many recipe books that were written at the time of their hegemony. Poems and recipe books alike celebrated the fragrance and savour of garlic. With their avid desire to experience new foods and absorb foreign

influences, and with access to the spices of the East, the cooks employed by the ruling Caliphs skilfully used garlic and onions to great effect in a dazzling repertoire which combined and contrasted many ingredients.

Garlic and onions have long played an important role in Russian cuisine, both as valued store vegetables and, together with dill and horseradish, as assertive flavourings to tone up plain ingredients, complementing the staples of bread, pickled cabbage, smoked fish, caviar, salt meat, soured cream, curd cheese and wild mushrooms, all washed down with a kind of beer called *kvas*.

Elsewhere in central and eastern Europe, garlic and onions have long figured prominently in the various national cuisines, especially as winter produce: for example, one Bulgarian speciality that is rather unlikely to appeal to western palates is a hefty salad of raw onions and garlic, dressed with vinaigrette.

Wel loved he garleek, oynons and eek lekes,
And for to drynken strong wyn, reed as blood

Despite Chaucer's description of such appetites as would befit a Spaniard, Italian or Frenchman, the traditional English dislike of garlic probably goes back a long way, although onions and leeks have been enjoyed in the British Isles for centuries. The ubiquitous 'ploughman's lunch' that is served virtually in every pub in the country, consisting of pickled onions, cheese, salad and bread, is a contemporary version of the traditional farmer's midday meal of home-baked bread, fresh onions and ale, and occasionally some cheese. The Welsh adopted the leek as a national emblem after King Cadwallader's forces adorned themselves with the vegetable as a means of identification, and succeeded in repelling and routing a Saxon invasion in 640. In England, however, the leek was always something of a last resort, appreciated in winter and early spring, when other vegetables were scarce.

That doyenne of Victorian housewives, Mrs Beeton, no doubt represented the sentiments of the majority when she wrote of garlic in her *Book of Household Management*, 'the smell of this plant is generally considered offensive'. It used to be the mark of a gentleman never to touch onion and garlic, perhaps because the vegetables were associated with the lower classes and with foreigners. This aversion remained the order of the day until the 1950s and 1960s, when Elizabeth David's first book, *Mediterranean Food*, began to transform the tastes of the British middle classes, and when package holidays opened the doors to an appreciation of Mediterranean food on a large scale.

In the USA the many immigrant nationalities have preserved to a greater or lesser extent their own distinctive traditional cuisines: southern Italian and Sicilian, eastern European, French, Chinese, and, latterly, Hispanic and Central American, and south-east Asian. Those North American cities with large concentrations of these communities offer perhaps the widest choice of different cuisines anywhere in the world, and all are accessible in the many restaurants and eating places that thrive there. Perhaps most interesting of all is how some of these influences have come together, for example, in the experimental way in which Mediterranean, Central American and Oriental ingredients and cooking techniques have helped to characterize the best Californian cooking today.

Although the Anglo-Saxon and Irish communities have tended to share the traditional English aversion to garlic, other, newer Americans have continued to enjoy it as a cornerstone of their own traditional cuisines.

The recipes in this book, culled from nations as diverse as Scotland, France, Spain, Italy, Greece, Turkey, India, Thailand and China, reveal just how deliciously versatile garlic and the other edible alliums are. All serve four, unless otherwise indicated.

PART TWO

PICKLED GARLIC

This pickle recipe from Vatcharin Bhumichitr's book *The Taste of Thailand* is intended to provide a sweet, sour and very pungent counterpoint to spicy southeast Asian curries cooked in coconut milk. Vatch admits that 'it is something of an acquired taste and one best shared with close companions!' The intended combination with Thai food is quite delicious, whatever the consequences.

2 large whole heads of garlic,
separated into cloves and
peeled
225ml/8fl oz/1 cup rice vinegar
2 tsp sugar
2 tsp salt

Put the garlic into a small glass jar with a tight lid.

Heat the vinegar with the sugar and salt until they are dissolved. Allow the mixture to cool, then pour it over the garlic, seal, and leave for a week before consuming.

ALLIOLI, AÏOLI, SKORDALIA

A little known and most impressive dish from the province of Alicante in south-eastern Spain is a kind of paella known as *Arroz Abanda*, made with a rich seafood stock (broth) and always served with plenty of *allioli* – which means 'garlic and oil'. This pungent garlic sauce is common throughout the western Mediterranean, especially in Valencia and Catalonia (where it is traditionally made without the egg yolks) and in Provence, where it becomes *aïoli*. From the opposite side of the Mediterranean comes a similar sauce called *skordalia* (*skordó* is Greek for garlic).

Variations include the addition of almonds or pine nuts or, if the sauce is to enliven baked fish, a little of the fish's cooking liquid and sometimes boiled potatoes to thicken the sauce. Egg yolks are frequently omitted. The basic sauce also suits barbecued marinated chicken, char-grilled or deep-fried vegetables, and *crudités*.

6 or more cloves of garlic (see note below)
salt
225ml/8fl oz/1 cup olive oil
2 egg yolks
1 slice of stale white bread, crumbed *or*
30g/1oz almonds or pine nuts (optional)
1fl oz/2 tbs lemon juice or 1 tbs of wine vinegar

Traditionally the ingredients are pounded in a pestle and mortar, starting with the garlic and salt, then a few drops of the olive oil, the egg yolks (at room temperature), the bread or nuts, more oil in a trickle until it has been exhausted, and finally the lemon juice or vinegar. The sauce should be thick. Equally good results can be achieved in a food processor: put the peeled cloves of garlic in the bowl with the salt, egg yolks (at room temperature), bread or nuts (if using) and very little oil. Blend until smooth, then add the rest of the oil in a trickle with the motor running, and last of all the lemon juice or vinegar.

Note: for a milder sauce use fewer cloves, or simmer them first for a few minutes in a little hot oil or boiling water.

Gambas al Ajillo
· · · · · · · · · ·

This is one of Madrid's most famous dishes, traditionally served piping hot in small, earthenware bowls with plenty of bread to mop up the flavoured olive oil. Raw (that is, uncooked) prawns (shrimps) are essential, whether fresh or frozen. Few other dishes are as simple and quick to prepare.

350g/12oz small raw prawns, (thawed, if originally frozen)
225ml/8fl oz/1 cup olive oil
4 fresh or dried red chillies, sliced or crumbled
3 cloves of garlic, peeled and coarsely chopped
handful of parsley, washed and chopped
salt

Pre-heat your oven at maximum setting. Put four earthenware ramekins in to heat. Shell the prawns.

Heat the oil in a large, seasoned cast-iron or non-stick frying pan. When hot but before it smokes, add the chillies, garlic and the shellfish. Stir around until done, 1–2 minutes. (Do not overcook or they will toughen up.) Sprinkle with the parsley and salt and divide the contents of the pan, oil and all, equally between the ramekins, handling these with a cloth so as not to burn your hands. Serve while still sizzling.

CHICKEN WITH GARLIC

Here are two quite different methods of cooking chicken with garlic: the first is typically Spanish, the second classically French, and both accentuate poultry's natural affinity with the fragrant bulb. If you rely on supermarkets, always choose corn-fed or genuinely free-range birds, which are usually far tastier than those fed on pellets.

Chicken with sherry and garlic

a whole oven-ready chicken
2fl oz/4 tbs olive oil
black pepper
6 cloves of garlic, peeled and lightly crushed, but left whole
pinch of dried thyme, or 2 fresh sprigs
110ml/4fl oz/½ cup fino or other dry sherry
generous handful of parsley
salt
juice of ½ lemon

Divide up the chicken into two whole breasts and legs. Quarter the breasts and, with a very sharp knife, cut away the leg meat from the bone. Save the carcass to make stock (broth).

Put the chicken pieces into a bowl and cover with the olive oil. Add a grinding of black pepper, the whole garlic cloves and the thyme. Mix thoroughly, cover, and leave to marinate for as long as possible, at least 2 hours.

When you are ready to start cooking, remove the garlic cloves and bring them to a steady simmer for 5 minutes with a little water to cover. Remove and reserve them.

Heat a large, well-seasoned or non-stick frying pan. Slide in the chicken, all the marinade and the garlic, turning to lightly brown all the pieces. Add the sherry, parsley and salt. Season again with a little more black pepper, cover and simmer on a reduced heat for 5 minutes. Uncover and add the lemon juice. Serve at once, accompanied by potatoes. The garlic cloves are meant to be eaten, but those preferring not to will still enjoy their influence without ruining their breath!

Poularde à l'ail

2 heads of garlic
a whole, cleaned roasting bird (the larger, the better)
some sprigs of fresh parsley, sage, rosemary and thyme, washed
freshly milled black pepper
110ml/4fl oz/½ cup olive oil
2fl oz/4 tbs water, or dry white wine
salt
1½fl oz/3 tbs brandy
a little more parsley, washed and chopped

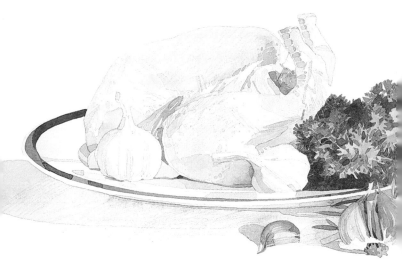

Pre-heat the oven to 200°C/400°F/gas mark 6

Divide the heads of garlic into cloves but do not peel them. Simmer them for 5 minutes in enough boiling water to cover them. Remove.

Stuff the chicken's cavity with the garlic and herbs and season all over with black pepper. Place on a roasting tin and pour over the oil and the water or wine. Roast for 30 minutes, basting occasionally, then turn and continue to roast for 45 minutes, turning once more. Towards the end of the roasting time, sprinkle the chicken with salt.

Remove the bird and leave it to rest for 5 minutes while you tip the juices into a pan with the brandy. Bring to a simmer.

Carve the bird and serve with the garlic cloves scooped from the cavity, surrounded by the thick sauce. Accompany with a vegetable and some thick rounds of lightly toasted or baked french bread on to which the sweet, tender garlic pulp can be squeezed out of its papery skin. Garnish with the parsley.

CHICKEN DOPIAZA
· · · · · · · · · ·

This subtle Indian dish of chicken with onions goes equally well with plain rice or an Indian bread such as nan or chappati. Accompany also with a dal, a spicy carrot relish and some mango chutney.

1 large roasting chicken, skinned
1 tbs whole cumin seeds
1 tbs whole coriander seeds
1 tbs fennel seeds
stick of cinnamon
6 cardamom pods, whole
8 cloves
4 dried red chillies, de-seeded
5 cloves of garlic, peeled
2cm/1 inch piece of fresh ginger, peeled
225ml/8fl oz/1 cup water
110ml/4fl oz/½ cup sunflower or other light vegetable oil
3 large onions, peeled, halved and thinly sliced
2 bay leaves
110ml/4fl oz/½ cup live, strained yoghurt, beaten
well with a fork
salt
freshly milled pepper
handful of fresh coriander (cilantro), washed
and chopped

Cut the chicken into leg and breast portions.

Grind all the dry spices in a clean coffee grinder, or pound them well with a pestle and mortar.

Roughly chop the garlic and ginger and put them and 2fl oz/4 tbs of water in another mortar and pound to a paste (or process in a food processor).

Heat half of the oil in a large saucepan and put in all the sliced onions. Stir around over a high heat for 5 minutes, then reduce the heat and stir around for 5 more minutes, until the onions have begun to turn brown. Remove and reserve them.

Add the rest of the oil, the bay leaves and the spices and stir them well. Put in the chicken pieces and stir them around for 3–5 minutes.

Add the ginger and garlic paste and cook that for 5 minutes. Return the onions, tip in the yoghurt, stir well and allow it to melt into the sauce. Add the remaining water, season and mix well. Cover, and simmer for 25 minutes. Now spoon off all the visible surplus oil. Mix again, garnish with the coriander and serve.

CHICKEN WITH GARLIC AND HOISIN SAUCE

This thick Chinese bottled sauce is made from soya beans, sugar, vinegar and garlic, and can be bought ready-made in Oriental supermarkets or grocery stores, sometimes labelled as 'barbecue sauce'. It usually accompanies Peking Duck, and is used here as a sauce for chicken stir-fried with garlic.

4 chicken breasts, skinned and cubed
2 tsp sesame oil
3fl oz/6 tbs peanut oil
1 tbs Shaohsing wine or dry sherry
salt
freshly milled black pepper
2 green chillies, washed
8 cloves of garlic, peeled
2 spring onions (scallions), washed
1 large carrot, peeled
1 stick of celery, washed
2fl oz/4 tbs hoisin sauce
75g/3oz cashew nuts

Combine the chicken in a bowl with the sesame oil and 2 tbs of the peanut oil, and half of the Shaohsing wine or sherry. Season, mix and leave to marinate for about 30 minutes.

Meanwhile, slice the green chillies. Chop the garlic and slice the spring onions thickly, separating the green and white parts. Slice the carrots and celery thinly at an oblique angle.

Heat the remaining peanut oil in a wok or large, steep-sided pot, put in the green chillies, garlic and white spring onions and stir. Then add the carrots and celery and stir-fry for about 3 minutes. Then tip in the chicken. Stir it around for 2 minutes, then add the rest of the Shaohsing wine. Stir. Add the hoisin sauce and cashews and heat thoroughly. Sprinkle with the green spring onion and serve with plain boiled rice.

Oignons a la Monegasque

An elegant dish from Monaco. Serve as a cold hors d'oeuvre.

450g/1lb very small onions, or pickling onions
335ml/12fl oz/1½ cups water
110ml/4fl oz/½ cup champagne or good white wine vinegar
1½fl oz/3 tbs extra virgin olive oil
2 tbs tomato paste
2 bay leaves
pinch of dried thyme (or a fresh sprig)
handful of fresh parsley
pinch of saffron strands
1 clove
salt
freshly milled black pepper
25g/1 oz seedless raisins
2 tsp sugar

Peel the onions and put them, whole, in a saucepan with the other ingredients. Bring to the boil, reduce the heat, cover and simmer for 25 minutes. Boil off the surplus liquid, then allow to cool and refrigerate. Serve chilled, with two or three other appetizers.

CHIVE AND PARSLEY OMELETTES

The herb of the allium family, chives are a versatile flavouring. The purple flowers that appear on the tips of the leaves are also edible and may be used to decorate salads.

9–12 very fresh free-range eggs (depending on size)
generous handful of chives
generous handful of parsley
1fl oz/2tbs olive oil
salt
freshly milled black pepper

Beat the eggs in four individual cups or little bowls.

Wash, pat dry and chop the herbs and combine them with the beaten eggs.

Heat ½ tbs of olive oil in a small, well-seasoned or non-stick frying pan and swirl it around. When smoking, tip in one of the cups of eggs. Swirl around to distribute the egg, season, and fold in half, allowing the egg to spread out. Turn and cook briefly on the other side, then turn again. The omelette is done when the centre is no longer runny, but still soft. Serve one guest while you cook three more omelettes.

Accompany with good bread and a salad of mixed spring leaves.

Spring Leaf Salad

Combine together generous quantities of at least five of the following leaves and shoots, except wild garlic or spring onion and sorrel leaves of which 4–6 will suffice.

flat-leaved parsley, stems removed
dandelion leaves (picked from tender young plants that
have not yet flowered)
sorrel or young spinach leaves
rocket leaves
lamb's lettuce (corn salad) leaves
wild garlic leaves, or green leaves of spring onions
(scallions), sliced
lettuce hearts
2fl oz/4tbs extra virgin olive oil
1fl oz/2tbs balsamic vinegar
½ tsp mustard
salt

Wash all the leaves, drain them and pat them dry with a paper towel. Arrange them, well mixed, in a glass or china bowl.

Beat together the extra virgin olive oil, balsamic vinegar, mustard and a little salt and pour over the leaves. Combine and serve at once.

PASTA WITH LEEKS
· · · · · · · · · · ·

Any chunky durum wheat pasta shapes are successful with this sauce: *rigatoni, penne, marille, lumache,
fusilli, farfalle, conchiglie,* or *ziti.* Serves 4 as an
appetizer, or 2 as a main course.

3 leeks, trimmed and well washed
1½fl oz/3 tbs olive oil
2 cloves of garlic, peeled and finely chopped
200g/7oz mushrooms, sliced
4 plum tomatoes (canned or fresh), chopped
110ml/4fl oz/½ cup water
salt
freshly milled black pepper
450g/1lb dried pasta
generous handful of fresh parsley, washed
50g/2oz parmesan, grated

Slice the leeks horizontally into 1cm/½ inch sections.

Heat the olive oil in a saucepan and add the leeks.
Sauté for 5 minutes before adding the garlic and
mushrooms. Sauté for 3 more minutes, then add the
tomatoes and water. Season well and stir.

Meanwhile, bring plenty of salted water to a rapid
boil in your largest pot. Add a drop of oil and the pasta
and cook for about 10–12 minutes, or until just soft.

While the pasta is cooking, simmer the sauce until
it has thickened, about 10 minutes.

When the pasta is ready, sprinkle the parsley over
the sauce, drain the pasta and combine the two, mixing
well. Serve from the hot pan, with freshly grated
parmesan and good bread.

LEEKS IN TOMATO SAUCE
· · · · · · · · · · ·

A dish of leeks prepared this way is suitable both as a vegetable accompaniment and as an appetizer. The leeks are sliced horizontally into fairly large sections to keep them from disintegrating.

6–8 medium leeks, washed and trimmed, outer leaves
removed
1fl oz/2 tbs olive oil
1 mild red chilli pepper, washed and sliced
200g/7 oz canned tomatoes, chopped
2fl oz/4 tbs water
1 tsp freshly ground cumin
salt
freshly milled black pepper
handful of fresh coriander (cilantro), washed and chopped

Slice the leeks horizontally into 6cm/2½ inch sections. Heat the oil in a pan and add the leeks and chilli pepper. Stir them well for a minute, then add the tomatoes, the water, cumin and seasoning. Cover, turn heat to low, and simmer for 15–20 minutes. Sprinkle with the coriander immediately before serving.

Lamb Braised with Garlic

Cooked this way, lamb is meltingly tender and richly satisfying. Serve, accompanied by a purée of potatoes or celeriac (celery root), or with steaming polenta, enriched with parmesan and a little butter.

900g/2lb leg of lamb
3fl oz/6 tbs olive oil
1 head of garlic, separated into cloves, peeled but left whole
1 carrot, peeled and sliced
1 stick of celery, washed and sliced
12 shallots, peeled and roughly chopped
560ml/1 pint red wine
1fl oz/2 tbs soy sauce
4 tomatoes, fresh or canned, chopped
2 bay leaves
salt
freshly milled black pepper

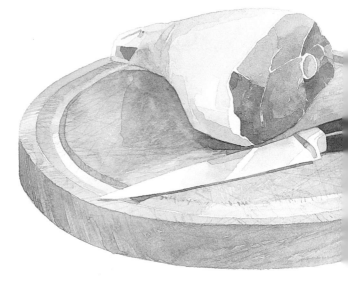

Trim the lamb very thoroughly of all visible fat and cut it evenly into cubes, ensuring that all are of equal size.

Heat the oil in a large saucepan, add the garlic cloves and simmer until they begin to colour, then remove and reserve them.

Brown the lamb in batches, then remove and reserve it. Soften the carrots, celery and shallots in the oil for 2–3 minutes. Return the lamb and garlic. Pour in the red wine, soy sauce and add the chopped tomatoes and bay leaves. Season, mix well, and bring to the boil.

Reduce to a low simmer and cook, partly covered, for 45 minutes to an hour, checking that the lamb does not dry out or stick to the bottom of the pan (remedy by adding a little more water). Serve.

TZATZIKI, CAÇIK

This is a wonderfully cooling *meze*, or appetizer, prepared with yoghurt, garlic and cucumbers that is popular all over the Balkans, in Turkey and even as far afield as the Indian subcontinent, in the modified guise of *raita*. Serve with crusty bread and *crudités*, some luscious olives and icy tumblers of ouzo, beer or white retsina.

1 medium or 2 small cucumbers, washed and peeled
225ml/8fl oz/1 cup Greek or other live strained yoghurt
½ tsp salt
2 cloves of garlic, peeled and very finely chopped
a little fresh dill or mint, washed and finely chopped

Grate the cucumber coarsely, then squeeze out as much water as possible in your hand. Set aside in a colander to drain further.

Beat the yoghurt in a bowl with the salt, then mix in the grated cucumber, garlic and the dill or mint. Cover and refrigerate. Serve chilled. (Do not keep for longer than 48 hours, and mix again before serving.)

Bruschetta

This is the original garlic bread, prepared with olive oil, not butter. You could also squeeze some juicy, ripe tomatoes over the bread and sprinkle with a little fresh basil.

1 loaf of Italian or french bread
2 cloves of garlic, peeled and lightly crushed
salt
extra virgin olive oil
2 large, ripe tomatoes, washed and halved (optional)
fresh basil leaves (optional)

Cut the bread into rounds about 2cm/1 inch thick. Toast them under a grill (broiler), or on top of a very hot griddle pan. Rub with the crushed garlic, sprinkle with salt and drizzle with enough oil, to soak through.

ORIENTAL EGG NOODLES WITH GARLIC
· · · · · · · · · ·

If you cannot obtain the fresh, oily, yellow noodles that are available in some Oriental stores, you can substitute dried Oriental egg noodles, reconstituted in boiling hot water. This is a slightly more elaborate version of a universally popular tangy street food. Vegetarians should omit the bacon or ham.

1 tsp peanut oil
2 eggs, beaten
6–8 spring onions (scallions), washed
175g/6oz oyster or button mushrooms
2fl oz/4 tbs peanut oil
6–8 cloves of garlic, peeled and sliced
2 slices of ham or lean bacon, trimmed and diced (optional)
4 fresh green chillies, washed
3 fresh or canned tomatoes, chopped
1 tbs sugar
juice of ½ lemon or 1 lime
1fl oz/2 tbs fish sauce or soy sauce
110g/4 oz bean sprouts
900g/2lb fresh *or* 1 packet dry egg noodles, reconstituted
1 lemon or 2 limes, quartered, to garnish
110g/4oz peanuts, crushed
2 dried red chillies, crumbled
handful of fresh coriander (cilantro), washed and chopped

Make an omelette with the beaten eggs and the oil. Remove and slice it into thin strips. Reserve these.

Trim the spring onions and slice them into small discs, separating the white and green sections. Slice the mushrooms.

Heat the oil in a wok or large saucepan and add the garlic. Stir once and add the white spring onion and the mushrooms, stir again and add the ham or bacon (if using), and the fresh chillies. When these start to brown, add the tomatoes, 2 tsp sugar, lemon or lime juice and fish sauce. Stir.

Now add half of the bean sprouts and the noodles and toss constantly for 1–2 minutes, to heat through. Transfer to a heated serving dish.

Arrange the remaining bean sprouts along the edges, garnish with the lemon or lime quarters, and sprinkle the peanuts, chillies, the remaining sugar, omelette strips, coriander, and green spring onions on top. Serve immediately.

STIFADHO
· · · · · · · · · ·

This excellent Greek meat stew with whole baby onions may be prepared with beef, veal or rabbit. If you cannot find tiny pickling onions, you can substitute larger ones, peeled and halved *horizontally* (this is important because if sliced vertically, they will separate into layers). The final addition of vinegar gives the dish its special tang.

110ml/4fl oz/½ cup fruity olive oil
900g/2lb tail end of beef rump, or braising steak, well
trimmed of fat and cut into large cubes (each about
4cm/1¾ inches)
900g/2lb (about 40) pickling or other small onions, peeled
4 cloves of garlic, peeled and chopped
2 bay leaves
2 tbs tomato paste
335ml/12fl oz/1½ cups water
2 cm/1 inch piece of cinnamon bark
salt
freshly milled black pepper
1½fl oz/3 tbs red wine vinegar

Heat the oil in a large, lidded casserole and brown the beef. Remove it and lightly brown the onions, taking care not to separate the segments. Remove and reserve them.

Return the beef and its juices, add the garlic, bay leaves, tomato paste, water and cinnamon. Season, mix and bring back to the boil. Cover, lower the heat and simmer very gently for 1½ hours. After 1 hour, return the onions to the pan.

10 minutes before serving, turn off the heat and add the vinegar, stirring gently. In tavernas and restaurants, french fries often accompany this stew, but any starchy accompaniment (rice, potatoes, noodles, or just plain crusty bread) will go well with *stifadho*.

Variation: sometimes pasta or potatoes are cooked in the stew, in which case more water is added.

Spicy Beef with Shallots

Southeast Asian influences have shaped this very tasty recipe. Use the best quality beef you can find, and trim away all visible fat. The bottled sauces are available from Oriental stores and supermarkets.

450g/1 lb beef rump or fillet
1fl oz/2 tbs thin soy sauce
1 tbs thick soy sauce
1 tbs fish sauce
1½fl oz/3 tbs peanut oil
4 crisp lettuce hearts,
washed and dried
(Little Gem are ideal)
4 or 5 shallots,
peeled and sliced into rings
4 green chillies,
washed and sliced
1 tsp sugar
1fl oz/2 tbs lime or lemon juice
1 tbs peanuts, crushed
4 spring onions (scallions),
washed and thinly sliced

Cut the beef into chunks, then slice them into thin strips. Combine with the soy and fish sauces and 1 tbs of peanut oil, mix well, cover and leave for at least ½ an hour.

Divide the lettuce hearts between 4 plates, arranging them concave side up, to receive the beef.

Lift the beef from the marinade. Heat the remaining oil in a wok or large non-stick pan. When the oil is beginning to smoke, add the shallots and stir-fry for 2 minutes. Add the beef and green chillies. Toss around to seal for 2–3 minutes. (The beef will give off a little liquid from the marinade.) Add the sugar and lime or lemon juice and serve sprinkled with the peanuts and spring onions and accompanied by plain rice.

Fried Aubergines (Eggplants) with Garlic and Yoghurt

This delicious Turkish appetizer is very quick and simple to prepare and might be part of a small array of tempting *meze*, together perhaps with a dish of hummus, green beans in tomato sauce, morsels of marinated and char-grilled meat, spicy little sausages, some olives, a salad of tomatoes and cucumbers, and chunks of feta cheese dressed with olive oil.

2 large or 4 small, slender aubergines, washed
225ml/8fl oz/1 cup Greek, or other live, strained sheep's-
milk yoghurt
pinch of salt
225ml/8fl oz/1 cup olive oil
2 cloves of garlic, peeled but left whole
1 tsp cayenne
handful of fresh coriander (cilantro),
washed and chopped

Dry the aubergines and cut them into discs about
1 cm/½ inch thick.

Beat the yoghurt with a little salt to a creamy
consistency.

Heat the olive oil in a large frying pan and sauté
the garlic until it colours a little. Remove and finely
chop it. Fry the aubergines in batches until golden and
drain them on absorbent paper. Allow them to cool and
arrange them on a serving platter.

Sprinkle each disc with a little chopped garlic, top
with a generous spoonful or two of yoghurt and finish
with a pinch of cayenne and a scattering of coriander.
Serve.

GAZPACHO ANDALUZ

Although other, paler, tomato-less versions of this excellent cold soup exist, this is what you are most likely to encounter in restaurants in Spain. One of the most famous of all soups, and arguably Spain's most successful gastronomic export, gazpacho is definitely best appreciated during the hottest summer months, not only for its icy temperature, but also to exploit the raw vegetables at their peak of condition. Certainly, at no other time will the tomatoes be good enough, although canned tomatoes can be substituted.

675g/1½ lb very ripe, red tomatoes, quartered
225ml/8fl oz/1 cup tomato juice
450ml/¾ pint/scant 2 cups water
110ml/4fl oz/½ cup fruity olive oil
1fl oz/2 tbs red wine vinegar
1 slice of bread, crust removed, in pieces
1 tsp sugar
1 white or yellow onion, peeled and chopped
1 red pepper, sliced
1 green pepper, sliced
1 cucumber, peeled and chopped
2 cloves of garlic, peeled and chopped
salt
freshly milled black pepper
2 slices of bread, crusts removed
1 green pepper, washed and trimmed of pith and seeds
1 white or yellow onion, peeled
2 tomatoes, washed
½ peeled cucumber

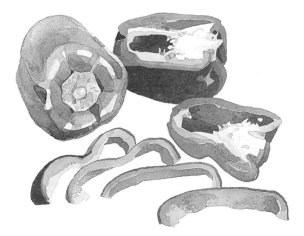

Combine everything except the last five ingredients in batches in the bowl of a food processor and process thoroughly and transfer to a soup tureen or large bowl. Chill for 2–3 hours.

Finely dice the bread, green peppers, onion, tomatoes and cucumber and transfer them to small bowls. Chill and float some ice cubes in the soup before serving with the diced ingredients.

COCK-A-LEEKIE SOUP

The name of this simple chicken and leek soup from Scotland is aptly descriptive. Best enjoyed in the colder months when leeks are plentiful and cheap, cock-a-leekie needs to be purged of the gelatinous fats imparted by the chicken. These will rise to the surface and can be removed easily with a spoon if the soup is cooled first and then gently reheated before serving.

6 large or 8 medium leeks, trimmed
1 chicken, all skin removed
2 litres/3½ pints water
salt
about 20 black peppercorns
several stalks of parsley with leaves attached
2 bay leaves
1 tbs sugar

Wash the leeks well, halve them vertically and cut them into segments.

Put everything in a large pot, adding water to cover. Bring to a boil and remove the scum. Reduce the heat and simmer for 30 minutes, removing any more scum from time to time.

Remove the chicken, take off the flesh and dice it into tiny cubes. Reserve this (you can keep some of it for another dish). Return the carcass, cover, and simmer for an hour.

Remove the carcass and all the scraps and bones and allow the soup to cool. Spoon off all the gelatinous fat before returning the soup to a simmer, mixing well. Now return the diced chicken flesh, re-season, and serve.

FISH SOUP
· · · · · · · · · ·

It is impossible to make a proper Marseillaise *bouillabaisse* without access to the local bony rockfish that give it its characteristic flavour. However, very good fish soups can be made with assorted Atlantic fish, such as cod, haddock, monk fish, skate, hake, red or grey mullet, as long as they are not oily-fleshed. *Rouille* is an orange, garlicky emulsion often served with *bouillabaisse*. Accompany with lightly baked rounds of french bread and a bowl of grated cheese.

900g/2lb of cleaned, mixed white-fleshed fish
salt
2fl oz/4 tbs olive oil
1 large yellow onion, peeled and chopped
white parts of 2 leeks, washed and thickly sliced
4 cloves of garlic, peeled and chopped
2 dried red chilli peppers, crumbled
1 carrot, peeled and chopped
1 small or ½ large red pepper, washed and diced
400g/14oz can tomatoes, chopped
2 tbs tomato paste
2 bay leaves
sprigs of parsley, thyme and marjoram
piece of orange peel
560ml/1 pint dry white wine
1600ml/2¾ pints water
½ tsp saffron strands
salt
freshly milled black pepper

Cut the fish into chunks and salt them.

Heat the olive oil in a large pan. Add the alliums, the chillies and the vegetables and sauté them over a high heat until they begin to colour (about 4 minutes). Add the tomatoes and tomato paste, the fish, herbs, orange peel, wine, water and saffron. Bring to the boil, cover, reduce the heat to medium and continue to boil for 25 minutes.

Remove the hard stalks of the herbs and the fish and all their bones from the soup. Separate the flesh from the skin and bones and reserve it, to make kedgeree or fish cakes. Discard the bones.

Strain the soup, return it to the pan, season well, and simmer for 10 more minutes.

Meanwhile, make a *rouille*, and bake the bread rounds. Serve with the bread, *rouille* and some grated gruyère, parmesan, or matured cheddar cheese.

Rouille

M ore fiery than *aïoli*, *rouille* goes well with any fish soup and can be prepared very successfully in a food processor, although purists would insist on pounding the ingredients in a pestle and mortar. It must share an ancestry with Catalan *romesco*.

140ml/5fl oz/⅔ cup olive oil
2 cloves of garlic, peeled
1 tsp cayenne
1 tomato, diced
1 egg yolk (at room temperature)
salt

Heat 2 tsp of the oil in a small pan and throw in the garlic and cayenne. Stir once and remove from the heat.

Combine everything except half of the remaining oil in the bowl of a food processor. With the motor running, gradually add the rest of the oil. Stop as soon as the sauce is thick and shiny.

Garlic Soup

N owhere in Spain is *sopa de ajo* so popular as in Castille, and specifically in the capital, Madrid. The rudimentary principal ingredients of garlic, broth, eggs and bread betray ancient peasant origins. Even the most urbanized of chic city revellers like to conclude a vibrant night out with a calming bowl of steaming garlic soup. Too substantial to precede a main course, this is a light meal in itself.

3fl oz/6 tbs fruity olive oil
6 cloves of garlic, peeled and very lightly crushed
4 slices of french or other crusty bread
2 tsp sweet paprika (*pimentón*)
pinch of saffron
1 litre/2¼ pints home-made chicken stock (broth)
2fl oz/4 tbs dry white wine, or sherry
salt
freshly milled black pepper
4 eggs

Pre-heat an oven to 220°C/425°F/gas mark 7.

Heat the oil in a large pot. Simmer the garlic cloves until golden, but do not burn them. Remove them and fry the bread. Remove it and add the paprika and saffron, stir, then pour in the chicken stock and wine.

Return the garlic cloves, season and bring the soup to a simmer. After about 5 minutes, carefully break the eggs into the soup and return the bread. Bake in the oven until the eggs have set, but before they harden (about 4 minutes). Serve each person one of the eggs and a slice of bread with a generous ladling of soup.

ONION SOUP
· · · · · · · · · ·

A satisfying and very warming soup for a cold winter's day. In this recipe, the onions are softened in olive oil, although traditionally animal fat is used.

3 large or 6 medium onions, peeled
2fl oz/4 tbs olive oil
1 clove of garlic, peeled and chopped
1120ml/2 pints home-made chicken or vegetable stock
(broth)
salt
freshly milled black pepper
4 slices of french bread
2 cloves of garlic, peeled
8 tbs grated cheese

Halve the onions vertically then thinly slice them to make long, narrow strips.

Heat the oil in a large pot and put in the onions and garlic. Partly cover, turn the heat to medium-low and simmer them for about 35 minutes, stirring occasionally to prevent them from sticking. They should now be very soft and lightly coloured.

Heat the stock and season the onions. Pour in the hot stock, mix well and bring to the boil. Cover, lower the heat and simmer for 30 minutes.

Meanwhile, make croûtons by slicing the bread into fingernail-size cubes, discarding the crusts. Heat the remaining olive oil in a small frying pan and lightly brown the remaining garlic cloves. Remove and discard them and toss the bread in the oil until golden. Remove and drain it on absorbent paper. Grate the cheese. Divide the soup between 4 capacious bowls and add croûtons and cheese.

Stir-fried Prawns (Shrimps)
· · · · · · · · · ·

A delicious Chinese way to prepare prawns, spiked
with garlic and spring onions (scallions).

6–8 spring onions, washed
3fl oz/6 tbs peanut oil
450g/1lb raw prawns, defrosted (if frozen) and shelled
8 cloves of garlic, peeled and finely chopped
3 green chillies, washed and sliced
2 tsp sugar
400g/14oz can of tomatoes, chopped
1 tbs rice vinegar
1fl oz/2 tbs Shaohsing wine
1fl oz/2 tbs soy sauce

Slice the spring onions into 2cm/1 inch segments and
separate the green and white sections.

Heat the oil in a wok and put in the prawns.
Remove them with a slotted spoon as soon as they
blush pink, and reserve them.

Add the white spring onions, garlic and chillies.
Stir, then add the sugar and tomatoes. Stir-fry for 5
minutes, to thicken the sauce, then add the rice
vinegar, Shaohsing wine, soy sauce, and return the
prawns. Cook for 1 more minute, then serve, sprinkled
with the green spring onion. Accompany with plain
rice and a stir-fried vegetable.

Romesco

A dried local variety of capsicum is used traditionally in this Catalan fishermen's sauce, for which recipes can be traced back hundreds of years. However, a combination of ground chilli or cayenne and Spanish sweet paprika (*pimentón*) works perfectly well. Individuals' special recipes for *romesco* abound but are rarely divulged. Some recipes in cookery books erroneously combine everything together raw: in fact, paprika needs to be cooked briefly, whether by roasting, grilling (broiling) or, as here, on top of the stove, with the tomatoes.

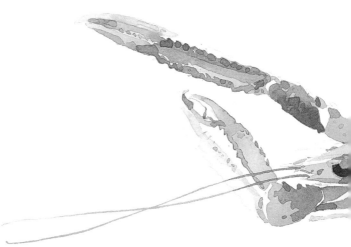

Romesco is served either to accompany seafood, or as the sauce in which it is cooked. This version is intended as an accompaniment to mixed fish and shellfish dipped in olive oil and cooked on a *plancha* (griddle) or in a very hot cast-iron frying pan, or lightly tossed in flour and fried in batches in hot olive oil.

225ml/8fl oz/1 cup fruity olive oil
6 cloves of garlic, peeled but left whole
50g/2oz split almonds
1 tsp cayenne
1 tbs paprika
2 ripe tomatoes, peeled and chopped (fresh or canned)
1fl oz/2 tbs red wine vinegar
2 tsp brandy
salt
sprig of parsley, washed

Heat about 1 tbs of the oil and gently simmer the garlic cloves in it for a minute, then remove and reserve them. Fry the almonds until golden, remove and reserve them. Add the cayenne and paprika, stir, and add the tomatoes, red wine vinegar and brandy and season with salt. Remove from the heat after 1 minute.

Allow the sauce to cool. Put it with the parsley and the reserved ingredients into a food processor. Process, slowly adding the remaining oil, until the consistency is smooth. This will keep for a few days in the fridge.

Steamed Fish with Garlic and Spring Onions (Scallions)
· · · · · · · · · ·

A classic Chinese method of cooking really fresh fish that works best with a small sea bass, although other white-fleshed fish such as sea bream or snapper are also suitable. This recipe will serve two people if served with plain rice, or four if served with rice and two other Chinese dishes.

whole fish weighing 450–675g/1lb–1½lb (cleaned)
½ tsp salt
1 tsp sugar
2cm/1 inch piece of fresh ginger, peeled and finely chopped
2 cloves of garlic, peeled and finely chopped
1fl oz/2 tbs peanut oil
2 spring onions, washed and thinly sliced
(white and green parts separated)
2 fresh red chillies, washed and sliced
1 tbs sesame seeds, lightly toasted in a dry pan
1fl oz/2 tbs soy sauce
1 tbs sesame oil

Rinse the fish and pat dry. Slash both sides with a sharp knife. Sprinkle inside and out with salt and sugar. Put it on a plate to fit inside a wok. Scatter the ginger and garlic over and around it.

Put a trivet into the wok and lay the plate on top. Pour in enough boiling water to come a little way up the sides of the wok, but staying well below the lip of the plate. Cover tightly with the wok lid, and steam over a low heat until cooked (15–18 minutes).

Carefully tip away the liquid that will have accumulated in the plate, or mop it up with absorbent paper.

Heat the peanut oil in a small pan, add the white spring onions, chillies and the toasted sesame seeds and pour the contents over the fish. Sprinkle with the soy sauce, a little green spring onion and the sesame oil and serve with plain rice.

STUFFED ONIONS
· · · · · · · · · ·

In Spain, onions and other garden vegetables such as peppers, tomatoes, potatoes and squashes are often stuffed; when some of these are served together, the name of the dish translates as 'stuffed garden'. You can replace half of the onions with peppers, blanching these with the onions.

8 medium onions, peeled, or 4 onions and 4 peppers
pinch of saffron
2 bay leaves
grating of nutmeg
2 cloves
2 cloves of garlic, peeled and chopped
400g/14oz can of plum tomatoes, chopped
2fl oz/4 tbs olive oil
salt
freshly milled black pepper
110g/4oz lean pork or bacon, diced finely
2 tbs pine nuts, lightly toasted in a dry pan
3 tbs breadcrumbs
1 cup cooked rice
4 tbs grated cheese
generous handful of parsley, washed and chopped
1fl oz/2 tbs white wine

Blanch the onions in a pan of salted water for 15 minutes. Remove and allow them to cool a little. Put the saffron, bay leaves, nutmeg and cloves into the water and simmer for 10 minutes.

Combine the garlic, tomatoes and 1½fl oz/3 tbs of olive oil in a pan and cook for 10 minutes, or until the liquid has reduced. Season.

Using a sharp knife and a spoon, cut around and scoop out the onion centres, leaving thin outer shells. Chop the centres roughly.

Heat 1 tbs of olive oil in a small pan and brown the bacon and half of the chopped onion centres. Remove them. Pre-heat the oven to 200°C/400°F/gas mark 6.

Make the stuffing by combining the pine nuts, bacon and onion mixture, 2 tbs of breadcrumbs, half of the tomato pulp, salt and black pepper, rice, parsley, and white wine. Mix everything thoroughly. Stuff the onions with the mixture and place them side by side in an oven dish. Top with the remaining tomato pulp and breadcrumbs, and the grated cheese. Stir the spiced blanching liquid and pour a little of it into the oven pan. Bake for 35 minutes.

BEAN SPROUTS STIR-FRIED WITH SHALLOTS
· · · · · · · · · ·

Serve this dish as an accompaniment to any of the Oriental main course recipes in this book.

1½fl oz/3 tbs peanut oil
1 tsp chilli bean sauce
8–10 shallots, peeled and sliced
350g/12oz fresh bean sprouts
salt
1fl oz/2 tbs soy sauce
2 tsp sesame oil

Heat the oil in a wok. When it starts to smoke, add the chilli bean sauce and the shallots. Toss them around for 30 seconds, then tip in the bean sprouts. Season, toss them for another minute, add the soy sauce and sesame oil, mix well, and serve.

POTATOES ROASTED WITH GARLIC

Like chicken, mushrooms and a few other ingredients, potatoes have a special affinity with garlic. Among many other garlicky methods of preparation, they can be sautéed with whole, peeled or unpeeled cloves and sage or rosemary, or thinly sliced and cooked in layers dotted with butter and finely chopped garlic and moistened with milk, or, as here, roasted with spices and whole, unpeeled cloves.

675g/1½lb all purpose potatoes
2fl oz/4 tbs olive oil or peanut oil
8 unpeeled cloves of garlic
1 tsp paprika
pinch of cayenne
a little dried thyme
salt

Heat the oven to 220°C/425°F/gas mark 7.

Parboil the potatoes in plenty of boiling water for 7 minutes. Remove and allow them to cool, then peel and halve them, or leave them whole if they are small. Roughen the surfaces by scoring them with a fork.

Place the potatoes in a large roasting pan and pour the oil over them. Turn them over, to coat thoroughly. Place them in the oven and after 15 minutes, add the whole cloves of garlic. Roast for 30 more minutes, turning once to brown evenly. Then sprinkle them evenly with the paprika, cayenne and thyme. Return to the oven for 10 more minutes to cook the spices. Season with a little salt.

Transfer the potatoes and garlic to a heated bowl and serve.

Variation: substitute whole, peeled shallots.

MUSHROOMS A LA BORDELAISE

Although in the Bordeaux area this is the traditional way of cooking wonderful firm young ceps (*boletus edulis*, king boletus), you can substitute cultivated *champignons*, preferably firm, organic 'brown cap', or 'Paris' mushrooms.

225g/8oz firm ceps or cultivated mushrooms
140 ml/5fl oz/⅔ cup olive oil
4 cloves of garlic, peeled and chopped
salt
freshly milled black pepper
2 handfuls of fresh parsley, washed
juice of ½ a lemon, or 2fl oz/4 tbs dry white wine
2 tbs home-made breadcrumbs

If you are fortunate enough to have bought or gathered young wild ceps, use a very sharp knife to shave away any hard, soiled bottoms. Clean them by brushing or scraping away any dirt and leave them whole if they are very small, or slice them thickly. If using cultivated mushrooms, trim off the very bottoms of the stems and leave them whole if they are tight buttons, or halve them.

Heat the oil in a heavy saucepan or seasoned frying pan and put in the mushrooms. Sear them for a minute or two then reduce the heat, and after about 5 minutes, add the garlic. Stir well and season. Continue to sauté for 5 more minutes, then add the parsley and lemon juice or wine. Increase the heat to reduce the liquid, and add the breadcrumbs allowing them to colour. Serve with a salad.

Stock (Broth)

Because some of the recipes in this book call for home-made stock, here are 2 simple recipes, one for chicken, the other for vegetable stock.

1 uncooked, skinned chicken carcass
2 large onions, peeled and quartered
2 large carrots, peeled and roughly chopped
1 large stick of celery, roughly chopped
bunch of fresh parsley (stalks and leaves)
12 black peppercorns
2 bay leaves
salt
2 litres/3½ pints water

Put all the ingredients into a very large pot and bring the water to a boil. Cover, reduce the heat and simmer, skimming off the scum from time to time. After 2 hours, the stock will be ready. Allow it to cool, remove any surplus fat and refrigerate or pour into freezer bags and store in the deep freeze until required. To thaw, pour boiling water over the frozen stock and carefully peel away the bag. Put the block of frozen stock into a pot, cover and simmer until completely melted.

To make vegetable stock combine in a large pot 2fl oz/4 tbs of olive oil, 2 peeled onions, 2–3 leeks, 3 carrots, 5–6 celery stalks, a parsnip, 2 tomatoes, some parsley stalks with their leaves, 1 tbs tomato paste, salt, freshly milled black pepper, and 2 litres/3½ pints of water. Bring to the boil, stir well, cover, reduce the heat and simmer for 1½ hours. Re-season. Store as above.

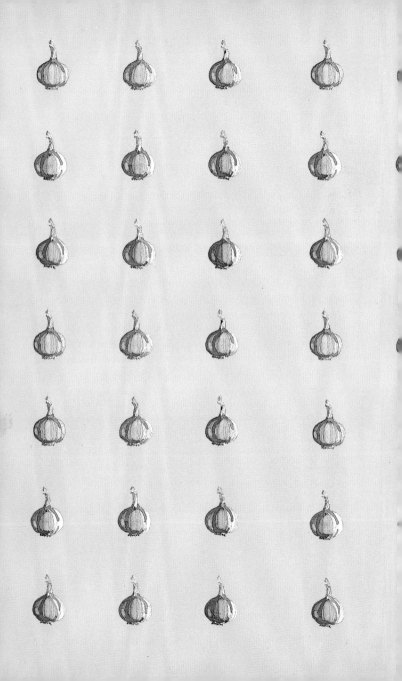